UNMASKED

the Power of
Courage and Vulnerability
to Live Free

No More Settling, Shame or Self-Betrayal

Katy Huff RN, BSN

UNMASKED

ISBN: 978-1-7357656-1-7 (eBook)
ISBN: 978-1-7357656-0-0 (paperback)
ISBN: 978-1-7357656-5-5 (hardcover)

This is a work of nonfiction. Nonetheless, some names, identifying and personal characteristics of the individuals involved have been changed.

"Can You Feel It?" song and verse by Angela Pinkston. Used with permission.
Scriptures noted marked (Amp) are from the Amplified Bible, copyright 1965,1987
Scriptures noted marked (NIV) New International Version Holy Bible. copyright 1973, 1978, 1984
Scriptures noted marked (NLT) New Living Translation Holy Bible, copyright 1996, 2004, 2007
Jared Emerson Artist copyright 2018 at jaredemerson.com, permission granted.

Printed in the United States of America.

First printing edition 2020

Katy Huff RN, BSN
243 Red Fox Rd
Lolo, Montana 59847
katy-huff.com/unmasked

CONTENTS

ACKNOWLEDGEMENTS

Thank you to my amazing husband, David Mortensen, who has been my greatest cheerleader to step into my calling and purpose. I am grateful for all of your unconditional love, grace, and encouragement as you walked beside me through this process. Your never-ending support and speaking life into me and my dreams has meant the world to me. You are my greatest gift from God, who is always faithful.

I would love to express my love and appreciation to my parents, Jim and Jean Huff, who are dancing in the streets of heaven with their amazing examples of being committed to working hard and following your dreams. Their faith and trust in God plus never give up attitudes has driven me to complete this book while hearing my father say, "my money is bet on you."

To all my spiritual sisters and brothers, who have encouraged me throughout this process. You have held me up, prayed over and for me as I ventured through my writing to be vulnerable in an effort to encourage others to set themselves free and live courageously.

Finally, my love and relationship with my heavenly father, Jesus, who has placed in me the desires of my heart and has never left me or forsake me in this process or ever. Because of His constant love, grace and plan for my life, I am humbled and grateful.

My sincere hope and prayer is that through reading this book that your lives would be enriched and empowered to live life UNMASKED, no longer hiding with shame, settling and self-betrayal. Ultimately, my greatest desire would be for you to know that you are loved unconditionally in all the decisions of your life.

Thank you for reading my book.
It is an honor and blessing to me. It
would mean the world to me if you
would write a review from where you
purchased it. I hope you will share and
recommend my book to your family and
friends.

To show my appreciation, I invite you to
sign up to receive my free workbook that
accompanies my book, **UNMASKED.** It is
my blessing to give this to you.

Please go to
www.katy-huff.com/freegift
and I will forward the workbook to your
email.

INTRODUCTION

HAVE YOU EVER been in a relationship thinking you have found "the one," only to wake up one day and realize you have settled? That is the day that you began putting on a mask--ashamed, embarrassed, humiliated and feeling unworthy--hiding behind it with your new motto being, "Fake it till you make it." Well, you are not alone! Unfortunately, we sell ourselves out for many reasons only to later realize we were betrayed by the one we thought was our knight in shining armor or "perfect" partner. Furthermore, you wake up one day with your heart crushed and realize you have also betrayed yourself by settling for someone whom you knew early on in the relationship you were not equally matched with—you ignored those red flags that were flying everywhere. You tell yourself, *I am a strong, independent, professional, faith-filled woman* and look past the signs, thinking, *I can make this work since, after all, the partner had all the qualities I was looking for in my mate for life.* Somewhere in your head you heard, "Run, Forest! Run!" and had a pit in your stomach. You reason with yourself that you have everything in common. However, the single most important quality that would be the greatest support for the relationship to last forever was missing!

The choices we make or the situations we find ourselves in cause us to want to put a mask on and run. Well, if this is you, then you can unmask, set yourself free, and *faith* it till you make it instead of faking it till you make it. You can be ok with not being ok. You can move from being broken to being blessed and living in the truth of who you are and whose you are. No longer selling out at the soul level and settling, yet having the courage to be vulnerable to set yourself free. Finally realizing you were betrayed and, more importantly, you betrayed yourself by settling for what has shown up and not paying attention to the red flags that hit you in the forehead.

This book will show you how to go from settling in relationships to having what you desire, deserve, and are called to be, do, and have in your life. You will be able to spot the red flags and stop before you sell yourself out. In order to experience anything worthwhile, like a relationship that lasts forever, you have to be willing to be vulnerable, and therefore, have the courage to be vulnerable and the power to set yourself free to live without a mask.

I have personally experienced settling and selling out at the soul level. I have spent years in a relationship I thought was *it* and have coached women to live life intentionally versus settling for relationships that cause you to sell yourself out. By reading this, you will gain super soul strength and recognize how to not question your worth based on what a man says or does to you but to set yourself up for having the most amazing, unconditionally loving relationship. I have been a caretaker as an RN for years, and I have moved into being a core taker and soul maker, which means I help you to know exactly who you are at the core and soul. You will learn what another person says about you doesn't define you. However, it does define *them*.

I promise after reading this book you will have learned who you are at the soul and core level. Your confidence, strength, and belief will be established in who you are and the plan that is for you, so you will know that settling is not an option. You are worthy and you matter, you are priceless, and you are free to live without a mask. Your soul core strength will be ironclad. No longer will you feel ashamed, embarrassed, guilty, betrayed, humiliated, rejected, or unworthy.

No more settling for just the frosting on the cake; you will know how to get the whole cake. The Cinderella syndrome that sweeps you off your feet with all the bells and whistles with the superficial, glamorous, materialistic romance happens fast and furious. But then at midnight, you find yourself in the pumpkin carriage with a frog that is so broken, wondering what happened to Prince Charming. It is said that if it's fast, it is fragile, but going slowly makes it solid in the end.

If you don't read this book, the brokenness, shame, self-betrayal, feeling unworthy, and fear will continue to rear their ugly heads, tricking you back into the dance of settling for heart-wrenching relationships that are empty dead ends. Read on to learn how you were created to have more than you can ever think or imagine . . . That you will feel free and at peace to live without a mask . . . That you will be courageous enough to be vulnerable . . . How to be ok with who you are without guilt, judgment, fear, or feeling less than the amazing person that you are. Your self-worth and self-esteem will be so strong that you will see the signs, know them, and not settle for anything less than what is divinely chosen for you. In fact, there is a saying that you know that you are with the right person . . . That in your brokenness you will realize that you are special, loved, honored, chosen, priceless, and forgiven for all the decisions, choices, and the feelings that you have that are causing you to hide behind a mask. I encourage you to walk in your truth, free and at peace with the beautiful, blessed, bountiful woman you were created to be. You are perfect as you are with your imperfections that you feel. Everyone has made mistakes, bad choices, and hidden with shame. However, I encourage you to step into your greatness with peace, joy, love, and freedom . . . UNMASKED!

LIFE WITH A MASK

THE MASK IS defined as "a covering of all or part of the face, worn as a disguise or to amuse or terrify other people." So, the $100,000 dollar question is: *Why do we hide behind a mask? What is the purpose of a mask?* Well, experts say we wear a mask for many reasons:

- to camouflage ourselves
- to disguise the "real" me
- hiding from all kinds of things and issues
- fear of being exposed
- shame
- guilt
- poor self-image
- feeling unworthy
- unloved
- failure
- being judged

- as a cover
- self-doubt

What we are doing when we are wearing the mask is covering the hurt, shame, guilt, feeling unloved, the poor self-image, and failure, and hiding. It all comes down to the brokenness that everyone has experienced at one time or another in their life.

What is the answer to the mask?

Well, we wear a mask to keep all things hidden and hope all our reasons for wearing a mask will never come to the surface or be exposed. That is, the "real me" that we fear. The fear of not being loved, not being accepted, not being forgiven. Fear of just being okay with who we are, where we have been, or what we have done, possibly even what we have *not* done.

We were not created to live a life of condemnation or judgment. We were created to be free! Free of shame, free of guilt, free of judgments, and free of comparison. We are all human, and that means we are imperfect in our flesh. The belief that you have to be perfect is a terrible cross to bear and a lie.

Perfection is defined as "being entirely without fault or defect, flawless." That's a crisis in itself to think one could be flawless. The reality is everyone has flaws!

To be perfect, flawless, or without fault is something I would *never* want to even attempt to be. It is beyond any effort I would want to embark on, and something that no person would ever be able to accomplish. When people attempt to be perfect only to find that we were not created to be perfect, that is when one may reach for their mask. The mask, of course, allows us to hide or to pretend that we are something that we are not; the grand facade will eventually be exposed. The one thing for sure is, eventually and always, the truth will set us free. Frankly, and I need to break it to you, there was only one person who was perfect, and he died over 2,000 years ago for our iniquities so we could be set free. No more guilt for the mistakes. No more shame. No more hiding for fear of judgment or criticism. No more hiding due to expectations. The fact that we had bad thoughts, words, or deeds we carried out and possibly or probably affected someone else's life and our own lives is something many of us have done at one time in our life. What we need to do is recognize that we need to forgive ourselves for our mistakes. Being okay with who we are is key. There is no need for a mask. No need to hide. No need for believing that we are perfect in the thoughts of our Father in heaven. We are in this together, and together we can support and love on each other without guilt or judgment, knowing we are loved unconditionally. There is not one person reading this who hasn't felt broken, fearful, hurt, unworthy, ashamed, untrusting, guilty and the list is long depending on the situation we have just experienced.

However, consider this: Wouldn't it be nice to have the courage to be vulnerable at whatever cost? To live a life unmasked? To be at peace with where you are, where you have come from, and where you are going? And therefore, able to know that on this journey called life there will be trials and tribulations and that we will make good choices and we will make bad choices? Sometimes we walk in so much fear that we don't make any choices, which can lead us to feeling paralyzed and depressed. We are then stuck. Sometimes we don't even know that we are stuck. Yet, we are not moving forward or backwards. So, then we find ourselves retreating into the cave and hiding. When we are in the cave, we shut out friends, family, and society out of the fear of making another bad choice or, worse yet, creating an environment for the battle in your mind to take over and control your thoughts. An idle mind is a doorway to all kinds of attacks on who we are and where we are in our life journey, and to comparing of ourselves to others, which gives the negative, demeaning thoughts and lies an opportunity to create even more dismay and trepidation of where we are at that moment. Those thoughts lead us down the spiral stairwell into depression and isolation, frozen in anxiety, guilt, shame, or fear of making a wrong decision.

According to many experts, when you make no choice, that is, in fact, a choice. You're choosing to stay where you are and not move forward. You feel like you are in cement with no way out, which is obviously a lie.

Therefore, you retreat and hide. The cave then provides a wonderful environment for the battle in your mind to totally play havoc on who you are and who your support is, and then embarrassment, shame, guilt, and paranoia start to play on your mind. Your self-image and self-worth are very negative, seeing only the darkness and battle, questioning where you are going and if anyone really cares about you. The debate of where you are and where you think you should be versus looking at how far you have come on your path called life continues.

We are all on a path or journey to live a life of freedom, peace, joy, love, contentment, and happiness. It is a God-given right that He wants us to have and enjoy. We get to have free choice of what we do, what we think, and what the plan is for our lives. As I said, we were not created for shame, guilt, judgment, or fear. The battlefield of the mind is real, and hiding with a mask or in a cave will never set you free. In fact, when you isolate and retreat to your cave is when the battle in your mind explodes. Taking a small, limited time to pause, reflect, and evaluate what has happened and how to make it better is totally different than hiding, retreating, and running away. I love what the late Jim Rohn has said: "I wouldn't sign up for that course!" The journey to freedom and peace is a day-to-day process. Having awareness of what you are thinking and how that is affecting you is the first step to healing.

However, the belief is if we just wear this mask, no one else will see our mistakes or the real us. Or if we retreat to the cave with no communication and block the outside world out for as long as it takes to capture our discrediting thoughts, when we come out everything will be okay. *Not!* Choosing to wear the veil or mask keeps us in bondage to the issues that we feel are so big and that will never go away. However, when we take off the mask and believe with all our heart that we are forgiven for everything—regardless of how big or small of a mistake we have made, the hurts we have, or the thoughts that take us captive—we are set free and in peace. Remember, all is forgiven, and it is forgotten. In fact, there is a scripture that states, "As far as the east is from the west, so far has he removed our transgressions from us." (Psalm 103:12) Imagine that for a moment and just pause . . . From the east to the west, we have had all transgressions removed. Once again, it is finished! It is done! Never to be remembered or brought up again.

There is no issue, past or present, that will not go away. The saying "this too shall pass" is one truth that I recommend for everyone to adopt. There is no hurricane or storm that will last forever. Just check the weather report; it is constantly changing. One thing for a fact is everything changes. Life is either getting better or not; however, hold on and it will soon change again.

Where I come from in my profession and career, it is common to say "fake it till you make it." My interpretation of that is to put on your mask, hide the truth, and pretend everything is great, your life is perfect, your work is perfect, everything is perfect. So, we pretend by putting up a smoke screen or a mask instead of being positive and honest about the blessings that we all have and the good to great things in our life while being transparent regarding the challenges we have faced or are facing. By being real, we allow others to also have the courage to be real. This creates a freeing feeling and peace about being in integrity and authenticity. There will always be challenges in our lives, and how we look at them will help us to succeed and overcome the challenges we will all have.

It is said that it's not what happens that matters, it is how you handle it. Or another way to look at it is, it's better to look at the cup half full than half empty. We need to recognize we live in an imperfect world, and it's okay to take off the mask and set ourselves free. Free to be the women we were created to be with our flaws and our accomplishments as well. So we can aspire to be the best we can be at that moment and on that day. Allow ourselves to be OK with not being OK in that moment. Fail forward by not giving in or giving up. I once had a t-shirt that said the definition of success is getting up one more time than you have fallen. That is a most simplistic example of success. There will be failures in everyone's life, and it can be so encouraging to others to recognize that the man on the top of the mountain didn't get placed there, he had to continue to get up and press on till he reached the top; in fact, you could look at it as failing forward.

We were created to be able to live free without faking it. Hiding behind a mask keeps us living a lie and stuck. There is a huge difference between having a positive outlook on life and looking at the cup half full versus faking it. The following action steps will help in creating clarity of where you have been and where you can grow going forward.

— ACTION STEPS —

1. Make a list of the times that you have fallen down or failed at something and you felt ashamed, embarrassed, rejected, or betrayed and hid behind a mask, pretending that you had it all together.

2. Next, take each one of the examples that you have written down and think about how you could have handled it differently without the mask. For instance, imagine what it would look like or how it would have felt to walk in your truth of the emotion that you were experiencing, the honest, raw truth of what happened and the feelings you had around that instead of hiding behind the mask. Take an

inventory of your internal feelings of not being in integrity with your feelings or being authentic of who you are, a child of God, and whose you are, a daughter of a king.

3. Replace those feelings with the truth according to the scriptures.

For instance,

"Do not be conformed to this world but be transformed by the renewing of your mind." (Romans 12:1–2)

"I can do all things through Christ who strengthens me." (Phil 4:13)

"As far as the east is from the west, so far has he removed our transgressions from us." (Psalm 103:12)

A gift for you

Because you are worth so much more than you realize! I believe in you! When you're done with this, I should read it too! :) XOXO From Mom

BROKEN to BLESSED

FOR ME, 2016 was a year to remember, and painfully, I would like to forget! It was an absolute turning point in my life. I remember being so broken because I saw all my dreams, plans, and my future come crashing down or, better said, go up in smoke.

I was broken, so broken inside. I thought I had found the man of my dreams, the one who I was going to spend the rest of my life with, when things blew up. Imagine having someone in your life with whom you had everything in common. We both liked skiing, working out, golfing, fishing, shooting guns, and music. We lived in the same city while he was going to college. He was romantic, financially solid, liked the same foods I did and eating out at the same places. He showered me with cards, flowers, gifts; he adored me, cherished me, supported me. He was so loving, romantic, generous, faithful, committed, protective, and participated in church with me and the list goes on. Like I said, the man of my dreams! In a matter of misunderstandings and serious issues, it blew up bigger than you could ever imagine. I was broken! My world was upside down.

When I looked around, I saw so many of my friends were broken also. Many of us were wearing the mask and pretending all was well, while looking for love in all the wrong places. Many of them compromised themselves so they would not be alone, setting themselves up for failure with the decisions they were making in the heat of the moment for immediate gratification. Remember the song "Looking for Love in All the Wrong Places" from Urban Cowboy in the 1980s? Or how about the movie "Top Gun"? Romance and the rush of adrenaline at its best! I'm dating myself now, but who didn't love those movies? They had romance, excitement, the rush and the thrill of the moment! Hoping to find a friend and a lover—how empty and sad that situation was for so many of us, my friends and acquaintances. It looked like this: sitting in a restaurant during happy hour hoping that someone would buy them a drink, hanging out and creating a connection while wearing the mask that everything was great and they had it all together, only to reveal later how broken it is.

When you compromise on who you are and on the plans that God has for your life, which by the way are perfect and so good, you are settling for the frosting and not the cake. You're in the broken place of wanting a relationship so badly that you put yourself in places that compromise your beliefs and values. Whether you're a man or woman, in the end your self-worth hits the toilet. This has been happening forever and at the end of the day or night, you realize how empty and lonely you are and you're still looking for love, meaning, and purpose. The long-lasting unconditional committed love everyone yearns for is still missing.

I realized this activity was creating a huge hole in my relationship with my fiancé. I was hanging out with my gal pals in these particular gatherings, without him, spending "quality" time with my friends. At least that is what I thought. However, that was a huge mistake for me and my relationship. I am very independent and thought I could hang with the gals without taking into consideration his feelings or his heart about these gatherings. However, I remembered that some experts say you become the average of the five people you're around the most. Holy moly! That was the two-by-four hitting me across the forehead. I had a come-to-Jesus talk with myself. It was a day of reckoning. If I continued where I was at and with who I was around, I would be bankrupt, an alcoholic, and settling for superficial love only to end up alone once again. How many times do you have to experience that before you say enough is enough? I am done with this song and dance!

The saying goes like this: "The definition of insanity is doing the same things over and over and expecting different results!" And there you are . . . *broken.* Then comes the wake-up call. If you are willing to answer the call and make the major changes needed, you become clear on what you are called to be and do, and aware of the abundant blessings that give you the courage and strength to become unstoppable, unmasked, and free. In that moment, you realize you have to get beyond yourself and surrender. The moment when you are on your knees crying or better yet flat on your face and so broken is when you know that this is NOT what you wanted for your life, and it surely was not His perfect plan for you.

I knew that I was not the dating type but the marrying type. Having my phone ring non-stop for different activities, to never be settled or at peace, always chasing the next activity, the FOMO (Fear of Missing Out) syndrome was exhausting me and affecting not only my spirit but also my soul. I had to make some drastic changes so I could have what I desired and deserved. I realized that my picker was broken. What that means is that I was picking the wrong people for the wrong reasons and finally realized that God's plan and picks for me would bring peace, joy, and ultimate fulfillment.

I made a conscious decision to change the places I went and the people I was running around with to get my dreams to come to fruition. It was like *cold turkey.* I changed everything with the grace of God and created some amazing friendships with individuals that are encouraging, inspiring, and living an abundant life of freedom. I no longer have all the interruptions and distractions, and the phone rings for different reasons now than it did back then.

I thank God every day that I woke up and reached out to some friends who had an escape plan for me at their condo in Florida. My dear, sweet, angel-like, loving, supportive friends invited me to come and get healed from my broken heart. Through the grace of God and His unconditional love, I spent a week in Florida learning what true love really was and what it looks like. I went to Florida with the intention of getting answers to my relationship that was broken, peace about the situation we were in, and miracles in our relationship. It's an amazing experience when you get what you are asking for. I was poured into like never before. I was surrounded by people who were such a blessing and so supportive of me and my situation. My dear friends also had been in a place of brokenness in their lives and their marriage in the past, yet through the grace of God, their commitment to each other and their love, and their perseverance and willingness to do the work needed to have the most beautiful, loving, respectful marriage, they are now thriving in their marriage and life, all based on biblical principles. I say all this because there is not a person alive who has not been broken and who hasn't been through hell and back, who is wearing that mask saying everything is great and wonderful yet continues to march around that mountain over and over, until finally they surrender. They find grace, mercy, restoration, reconciliation, forgiveness, and a new beginning with a different outcome, which I call a beautiful restart. When you finally get to the end of thinking you can do it alone and look up is when everything changes. The perfect plan for each of us is good, and with the right timing, trust, and patience, all things will be given unto us.

Grace is defined by the free and unmerited favor of God and the bestowal of blessings. Isn't it amazing that even when you are feeling so broken and at your worst, that is when you get that two-by-four hit across your head moment and turn from the lifestyle of emptiness by means of your choices to one that is full of peace and joy? That is one of the greatest blessings and breakthroughs a person can ever ask for and receive. Even in your lowest times, there is grace and mercy. Mercy is compassionate and forgiving. You see, when we pause and reflect on where we are versus where we want to be, it is easy to see that even in our state of brokenness and with wearing our masks, we can move to a place of being blessed and free. Once again, that wonderful definition pops up: Insanity equals doing the same thing over and over again and expecting different results. The great "a-ha" moment: turn away from wearing a mask and pretending everything is great, and turn toward having the courage to say enough is enough. The courage to be vulnerable. I'm taking the mask off. I am not going to continue to do the same things and expect different results. I'm going to stop the madness, stop the insanity, and run to grace, mercy, and the loving open arms of God, knowing that I know that His plans for me are good. Jeremiah 29:11 is one of my favorite scriptures: "For I know the plans I have for you, declares the Lord, plans to prosper you and not harm you plans to give you hope and a future."

As I sat in this program, two people spoke the truth, light, and love into me, giving me hope. It was a life-changer. I knew that my dreams and desires were amazing. I knew I had to make a choice. The choice was so easy and simple at that moment. Did I want to continue in my brokenness or take the mask off, acknowledge where I had been, and to have the courage to live the life I desired? One life full of grace, mercy and blessings, knowing that my future was so bright. The great awakening for me was when I leaned on Romans 4:17–20: "God who gives life to the dead and calls into being that which does not exist. Without becoming weak in faith, she did not doubt or waver in unbelief concerning the promise of God, but she grew strong and empowered by faith, giving glory to God, being fully convinced that God had the power to do what he had promised." What that meant to me was God can do all things and even create miracles, like raising the dead and make things exist that didn't. Yet it takes *faith* with a capital "F" and no doubting, giving thanks to God, trusting and knowing without a shadow of a doubt that God would come through with His promises. Like the scripture states*: Being fully convinced that God has the power to do what He had promised!!* After all, if He can make the lame walk, the blind see, and raise the dead into life, then I had *no* doubt that He could create that miracle for me. That, my friends, is a *powerful*, life-giving, and amazing promise. It became like a mantra for me. The other scripture that was so impactful and encouraging for me is, "I can do all things through Christ who strengthens me." (Philippians 4:13) So we call on God's strength because He can do all things. What a relief that we don't have to have the strength to do it ourselves or rely on our own strength, but He can do all things. So grateful for that which gives us peace in knowing this is TRUTH!

I pray for all of you that you will walk away from the brokenness and emptiness and toward all the blessings that are waiting for you . . . That you will realize you are loved unconditionally and that we are forgiven . . . That the mistakes we have made are in the rearview mirror. We are blessed and we get second, third, fourth, fiftieth, or even hundredth chances to just start again. We have endless forgiveness because He loves us unconditionally. The scripture Psalm 103:12 states, "He has removed our mistakes as far from us as the east is from the west." Therefore, we get to press on to the plans and desires we have that God has placed in us. What God brings us to, He will bring us through. God is good, and he wants only the best for us. That is for us to be blessed, to forgive ourselves, to learn the lesson, and to make the decision to love ourselves as God has loved us, with grace, forgiveness, and mercy.

We are all on a journey of constant and never-ending improvement. I love what Joyce Meyers says: "I may not be where I need to be, but I thank God I am not where I used to be." Praise God for that, right? Every day is a new beginning. We get to start again when we come to realize that we will make mistakes, and there is no reason to hide behind the mask because we are forgiven. There is not a person walking that has not made bad choices. The accomplishment is when we stop the madness and turn 180 degrees knowing we are blessed and leave the brokenness behind. Remember when Jesus said, "You are forgiven, now sin no more"? Again, I have to repeat, He forgives us as far as the east is from the west. He is merciful and wants only the best for us. In fact, when we continue to bring up the same old issue to Him, He says, "I don't know what you're talking about." He's not only forgiven us, but He's also forgotten it. So then doesn't it make sense that we should forgive and forget as well? After all, if He's our teacher, our Father in heaven, then let's learn from the best and set ourselves free, which means walking in joy, peace, love, and freedom. His blessings are new every day, and we have been given grace and mercy. What an amazing, loving Father we have.

I want to share with you an incredible, encouraging thought of God's plan for us that prayerfully will inspire you.

> "Setback is a setup for a comeback. If God showed you all that He has planned for you, it would boggle your mind. If you could see the doors He's going to open, the opportunities that will cross your path, and the people who will show up, you'd be so amazed, excited, and passionate, it would be so easy to set your mind for victory. That is what faith is all about. You've got to believe it before you see it. God's favor is surrounding you like a shield. Every setback is a set up for a comeback! Every bad break, every disappointment and every person who does you wrong is part of the plan to get you to where you are supposed to be." — Anonymous

— ACTION STEPS —

1. Take a minute and write down the times you put your mask on to hide from the hurts, the betrayals, the rejections, the guilt, and all the emotions that made you feel unworthy, judged, or criticized.

John 8:7 states in the Bible: "He who is without sin cast the first stone." Well, no one is throwing any stones.

Or perhaps you've heard, "People living in glass houses shouldn't throw stones." What this means is *no one* is without mistakes! *Not even one!*

2. Next, recognize what was happening in your life at that time. What was happening in your life that caused the feelings you had? Where were you coming from? Were you hurt, feeling insecure, comparing yourself to others, feeling shame, needy, alone, etc.? What caused the brokenness that you felt the need to do what you did?

What was going on in your head in that specific situation?

Look back and reflect so you can forgive yourself and let it go once and for all. After all, if we are forgiven, then leave it in the rearview mirror where it belongs. Trust the fact that you are loved unconditionally through the good, the bad, and the ugly, and that you can be restored to wholeness, never needing to wear your mask again.

"Therefore, if anyone is in Christ, he is a new creation; the old things have passed away; behold new things have come." (2 Corinthians 5:17)

What this means to me is you are a new creation now that all the old things that were holding you back, causing you pain, shame, heartbreak, and settling are all gone. Get ready because new things are coming!!!

TRUTH versus EGO

THE TRUTH WILL set you free.

Truth . . . what is it and what does it look like? Truth is defined as "the body of real things, the state of being the case, fact."

Being transparent can be scary for many people. Why is that? Where do you start with this, right? Now that is a long list! The things that I hear—from so many—boil down to this: *By being transparent, I will feel ashamed of my choices, which leads to feeling unworthy, judged, criticized and unloved.* The lies in our own mind are what keep us up at night. The truth is we all have skeletons in our closets, and that is where they belong. There is no reason to relive, rehash, or even discuss them ever again. Let's put it this way: if the horse has been dead ten years, then it's time to dismount! The past is in the rearview mirror. What those experiences are there for is to provide empathy and sympathy for someone else that may be going through the same thing and allow you to give them grace as you would want to have from others. The Golden Rule applies here, to treat others like you would want to be treated. Wouldn't it be nice to know that when we fall down, which we will again because that is our humanity, then there will be someone there to empathize and extend grace and mercy to us also? And that they will be there to support us?

Let's take a step back and review some truths.

You are a child of God. *Truth.*

You are loved unconditionally. *Truth.*

You are forgiven, 100 percent. *Truth.*

As far as the east is from the west, our wrongdoings are forgotten. *Truth.*

You are worthy. *Truth.*

His plans for you are perfect. *Truth.*

You are the apple of His eye. *Truth.*

He will never love you more than He does right now. *Truth.*

You are His loving daughter or son. *Truth.*

He will never leave you or forsake you. *Truth.*

No weapon formed against you shall prosper. *Truth.*

And the truth will set you free!

Knowing now what is known as truth, one has to ask if the voice in your head, the one that you rewind and listen to over and over, is the truth or is it the ego. EGO stands for *Edging God Out!* It is defined as a person's sense of self-esteem or self-importance. Do you know how that looks?

Experts declare that when someone has a big ego, they

- never compromise, even if it is healthy and of mutual benefit.

- do not accept failures and are always defensive.

- negatively compare themselves to others as competitors.

- forever crave respect and recognition from others.

- get their identity from what others think of them and thrive on it.

- always showcase themselves.

- never sincerely accept and respect others or achievements of others.

- are never sincerely thankful and grateful.

And finally, if the person is outwardly arrogant, bragging, boasting, and very defensive in nature, then the person is struggling with ego. It is a sign of lack of self-confidence.

I find this very interesting, that the mask being worn shows outwardly as arrogance when deep down it is lack of self-confidence and insecurity, so they overcompensate with bragging and boasting.

It is their belief that they can handle it all on their own, or they don't need anyone else's help, that their ways are the *only* way. They think, *I have it all figured out, and it's all about what I can do on my own.* That's saying, "It's all about me, what I've accomplished, where I've gone, what I have, and material things," right? Joyce Meyers always uses her "robot" example. She marches around on the stage saying in a robotic voice, "WHAT ABOUT ME? WHAT ABOUT ME? WHAT ABOUT ME?" That couldn't be further from the truth. That it is all about you is not remotely close to the truth.

Proverbs 16:18 states, "Pride goes before destruction and a haughty spirit before a fall!" Now in the Message translation, it is even better: "First pride, then the crash—the bigger the ego, the harder the fall." Boom! That right there is a drop the mic moment! That, my dear, is very clear!

When we get to the end of ourselves and realize we can't do it alone nor do we want to, that's when we will hear, "I am here, I've got this, and I've been waiting for you with arms stretched wide open," like the loving Father He is. He wants you to talk with Him, pray to Him, lean into Him and have a relationship with Him.

We have free choice, yet the plan for us is so good! Why would we ever want anything less or settle? That, my friend, is the greatest love of all. Jesus, who looks at us as his dad looked at Him with such love in his eyes, adoration, forgiveness, and cherishing Him. He so loved the world that He gave His only begotten son. Wow! Can you even fathom that? It's so enormous in understanding just how *big* His love is!! Ephesians 3:20 declares, "Now to Him who is able to do immeasurably more than all we ask or imagine, according to His power that is at work within us." That is beyond my wildest imagination that He can and will do *immeasurably* more than our greatest wishes. How exciting is that for us? So, whatever dreams we have, we can count on the fact and truth that He will do more than we can imagine. Be so grateful for His unconditional love. This is when we have to trust that this is truth which will set us free. It doesn't say it "might" or "possibly" or "if you do everything right" or "it is conditional on what you do or say." It states that it *will* set you free! No more chains of guilt, shame, self-betrayal, settling, pain, humiliation, worthlessness, or embarrassment! You are set *free!* What a blessing it is to be able to remove the piano that you feel is on your back and *live light and free!*

> "So Christ may dwell in our hearts through faith and I pray you, being rooted and grounded in love, may have power, together with all the saints, to comprehend the length and width and height and

depth of his love and to know the love of Christ that surpasses knowledge that you may be filled with all the fullness of God." (Ephesians 3:17–19)

That verse always chokes me up due to trying to comprehend the length, width, height, and depth of His love. After all, He did and continues to do for us, to show us how much He loves us without conditions, and that is so *huge!*

Imagine that, or can you? Can you comprehend a love that is "the greatest love of all?" One that is the length, width, height, and depth that surpasses all understanding? The fact that He is our protector and provider, counselor and comforter; that He will defend us and even die for us; that there is no one like Him or will ever be again? Therefore, I ask again, why would we hide behind a mask? If we truly believe that each of us is a child of a king who wants nothing but the best for us, then we can be unstoppable. Not because of who we are, but because of who He is. When we believe who He is, it will set us free to live in the truth, plus have the courage to be true, the courage to be vulnerable, and inevitably, free to be who we are!

When a person lets go of the ego and humbles themselves, they will be setting themselves free to live in the truth, unmasked.

There is no greater truth than the unconditional love that He has for us. His plans for us are greater than we could ever imagine. His love for us is immeasurably more than we could ever imagine. That is the greatest peacemaking statement anyone could ever hear. The greatest comfort one could know is the truth that we are loved beyond measure and totally forgiven for any and all things that we may have done. That is freedom and peace, and therefore, living without a mask.

— ACTION STEPS —

1. Write down a time when you felt like you needed to boast or brag about what was happening in your life. For instance, an achievement or an award, or even a sporting event you were involved in, or a milestone with the company you worked for.

2. Describe an achievement that you received. How did you describe your achievement to those you shared it with? Did you come from a state of humility or one of ego? How would it sound if you came from a humble state? Can you see the difference of the truth versus ego?

3. Now state some affirmations aloud about yourself in those situations that can replace the feelings of inadequacy or low self-esteem. For example:

   • I am a child of God.

   • I am loved unconditionally.

   • I am more than enough.

   • I can do all things through Christ who

strengthens me.

- I am forgiven.
- I am courageous.
- I am free.

Finally, remember what others think of you doesn't define you. What does define you is that you are chosen, you are forgiven, and you are *free!*

FAITH OVER FEAR

"Do not fear, for I have redeemed you; I have called you by name, you are mine." (Isaiah 43:1)

FEAR IS DEFINED as "False Evidence Appearing Real." That is what fear stands for, false evidence. Remember this whenever fear lifts its lying head and plays games on your mind like a snake that wraps around your neck causing you to choke out, suffocate, and fall to the ground, breathless and unable to move, lying in a fetal position. It's false! It's a lie! It tries to distract you, paralyze you, and stop you from moving forward. You were created for greatness and to settle for anything less would be a tragedy for you, your family, and the community that you live in.

We've all had experience with fear. If only we would pause and change the radio station that is playing in our heads so that we remember the person we were born to be and the incredible plans for our lives, then fear will not win. In fact, Deuteronomy 31:8 states, "He will never leave us or forsake us. Do not be afraid, do not be discouraged." The presence of our Father holding us in his arms, protecting us and comforting us, is life-giving. It will extinguish any and all fear. He is always there, always loving and forgiving. He is our shield of protection that will whisper in our ears, "I am here for you. I've got this. Rest in my arms, my beautiful child. You are mine."

So, here's a challenge. Think back to when fear took over you. What was going through your mind? What was happening? Was it: *Will I lose my job? Will he or she leave me? Will I be alone forever? Will I be able to survive without him or her?* Heart-crushing, paralyzing fear plays on our minds and escorts us back to the cave where we are isolated because we feel we can't move forward. And one of the worst places to be at this time is in the cave. The choices come up. Do you continue to hide? Running back into the cave and isolating yourself opens a door for you to be attacked in the battlefield of your mind. Taking time to recoup and recharge is different than isolating oneself and allowing in the enemy who comes to steal, kill, and destroy, and who will do just that. It is imperative that you put on the full armor of God, so you can stand against your enemies. "The full armor of God is putting on the belt of truth, which sets you free and the body armor of God's righteousness. For shoes, put on the peace that comes from God so that you will be fully prepared. In addition to all of these, hold up the shield of faith to stop the fiery arrows of your enemies. Put on salvation as your helmet, and take the sword of the Spirit, which is the word of God." (Ephesians 6:13–17) Therefore, you can take your stand against your enemies' schemes. The battlefield of the mind is real. It will tell you lies and create a feeling of doom and gloom. It will tell you that you will never get out of the situation you are in, that you are unworthy, unlovable, unforgiven, and that you will never succeed or have another relationship. All of these are *lies, lies, lies!*

Or you may choose another path: put on the mask and pretend all is well, fake it, and hide. Smile through the pain and live a lie due to the facade you want to portray and the embarrassment of acknowledging that once again your relationship did not work out. The shame, embarrassment, humiliation, and guilt raise their ugly heads and cause you to want to run, put the mask on and pretend that with time no one will ask or even care. All the time, you feel like you are dying inside, yet in the quiet still of the night, you hear a voice that tells you, "I will never leave you or forsake you. Do not fear, it is I that goes before you. I will protect you and hold you in my victorious right hand." The love of God for us is never-ending. In Song of Solomon 2:10, it states, "My beloved spoke and said to me, 'Arise, my darling, my beautiful one, come with me.'" He is always there waiting for us to come home and to rest in His loving arms. Hebrews 13:6 reminds us, "The Lord is my helper, I will not fear." Or my favorite is Philippians 4:6-7, "I will not be anxious for anything, but through prayer and petition with thanksgiving, I will present my request to God. And the peace of God, which transcends all understanding, will guard my heart and mind in Christ Jesus." These scriptures are the armor we can use to verbalize, to create a wall of protection, and to create a mantra that changes our fear into faith, knowing, and declaring, "I can do all things through Christ who strengthens me." (Philippians 4:13) When we take off the mask again and walk in faith, we stop the fear and darkness by proclaiming light and life in all situations. Faith can and will prevail in any and all situations. Faith will set us free. Faith stops fear in its tracks. 1 John 4:18 states, "There is no fear in love, but perfect love casts out fear."

What does faith look like to you? Faith, for me, is believing and trusting that all things happen for a reason. That the timing of everything is perfect. Faith according to Hebrews 11:1: "Faith is the substance of things hoped for, the evidence of things not seen." Walking in faith is trusting that whatever you're hoping for will happen. Even if you aren't seeing it come as fast as you would like, God's timing is perfect all the time. 2 Corinthians 5:7 states, "For we walk by faith, and not by sight." Letting go of control and trusting that what you desire will come to pass.

I remember when I thought I was walking in faith only to find out the hard way that I wasn't. I felt like I was supposed to be in a city working and believing I would run into a friend I had not seen in quite a while. Hoping, praying, and believing that I was called to be there. A sure sign of stepping in front of faith and God's perfect timing is when you snatch control back of what you are wanting to happen and forcing things instead of letting go and letting faith arise. For an example, picture this: Have you ever seen a kite flying and soaring in the sky only to see it come crashing down to the ground like a yard dart? And I mean crashing where the kite explodes? Well, that is what happened to me.

The first sign of not walking in faith is when there is no peace. It is like being in the wrong place at the wrong time. You're sitting and waiting to see that person, client, friend, or past relationship and the whole time you have anxiety. Your insides are doing cartwheels, and you're shaking like a leaf. Then in a moment's notice, just like on the set of a movie scene you hear "ready, set . . . ACTION!" Now you are "on," or rather the mask goes on. You pretend everything is great, that you were meant to meet up and have a conversation, that it was a coincidence that you were at the same place at the same time. However, the reality is the conversation doesn't go as planned. You get kicked in the gut. You have betrayed yourself, once again thinking that this toxic relationship is what you're meant to have. When we don't rest in faith and trust that God has it all planned out and you step in front of His plan for yourself, it comes crumbling down around us like when Humpty Dumpty had a great fall, and we couldn't put all the pieces back together again.

In the next scene, the mask comes off and, through the grace of God, He gives us that "do-over." He picks up the pieces, dusts us off, and tells us, "I will never leave you or forsake you. My plans for you are good, just trust in me and my perfect timing. I promise you the desires of your heart will come to pass." In Habakkuk 2:2–3, it states, "Write the vision and engrave it plainly on tablets. So, the one who reads it will run. For the vision is for the appointed time. It hurries toward the goal of fulfillment; *it will not fail.* Even though it delays wait patiently for it, because it will certainly come; *it will not delay.*" Wow! He is so good! It can be a difficult challenge to just rest, let go, trust, and know that He will always provide and He knows what's best for us. After all, His plan for us is *perfect.* Our timing, unfortunately, is not His timing and His ways are not our ways. Yet, He always comes through, as it states it will not fail and it will not delay! On the eleventh hour, 59 minutes, and 59 seconds it will certainly come to pass. *Amen!*

Still, the staticky radio station in our head continues to play games, telling us all kinds of lies.

For instance:

> *You can't do that.*
>
> *You're not worthy.*
>
> *You will never accomplish that.*
>
> *You are alone.*
>
> *You should be ashamed.*
>
> *You will be exposed.*
>
> *You are a failure.*
>
> *What will people think of you?*
>
> *You're not qualified.*
>
> *You're unloved.*
>
> *You're not good enough.*
>
> *You're not pretty enough.*
>
> *You're not tall enough.*
>
> *You're not thin enough.*
>
> *You're not talented enough.*
>
> *You're not short enough.*
>
> *You're not smart enough.*

All of these lies create fear and paralyze us. When you hear this station play and lies rise up, change the station. Call them out and declare, *"Cancel! Retract!"* Turn the station! Stop the lies and the battle in your mind.

Replace these lies with the TRUTH:

You were created in the image of the one and only perfect man, Jesus.

He knew you in the womb and created you.

You are loved unconditionally.

You are forgiven seven times seventy, as far as the east is from the west.

You are a daughter or son of God.

He has a plan for you, and it is perfect.

His plan is to prosper you and to give you hope and a future.

You are redeemed.

He knows the desires of your heart and will bring them to pass.

You are forgiven.

It is our job to forgive ourselves. We need to trust in the process and perfect timing. To rest in the valleys, knowing we are never alone, and trust that all things are possible to those who believe. Psalm 23 states, "Even though I walk through the valley of the shadow of death, I will fear no evil, for you are with me; thy rod and staff, they comfort me." Therefore, we will once again be back on top of the mountain. At that point, we can look back and say, "Thank God I'm not where I used to be, and I am grateful for where I am today." Each day starting again, new, with constant and never-ending improvement.

He knows the desires of your heart, and He will bring them to pass.

Finally, remember *"the truth will set us free."*

We can and will do all things through Christ who strengthens us. (Philippians 4:13) It is HIS strength we call on and lean into, not our own. His strength is never-ending. Therefore, there is nothing that can stop us. Nothing! Fear is a liar! Fear steals your breath, your peace, your rest, your happiness and faith. So, when we are faithless, He remains faithful for He cannot disown himself. (2 Tim 2:13) He is faithful to the end of times. He is our great counselor and comforter, our provider and protector. We have to learn to lean on Him when we are feeling fearful and faithless because He will never leave us. This is the confidence we have in approaching God: that if we ask anything according to his will, He hears us. And if we know that He hears us—whatever we ask—we know that we have what we asked of Him. (1 John 5:14–15)

One of the most important things to remember is fear and faith cannot co-exist, so I recommend that we always choose faith over fear! When you have the feeling of fear, pause and say, "BUT GOD!" He is in the middle of the situation, and we can rest in knowing He never leaves us or forsakes us. He is always by our side.

"Now faith is the assurance of things hoped for and the conviction of things not seen." (Hebrews 11:1)

When we continually turn to the power of prayer and have faith in prayer, we can and will move mountains. There is so much evidence and proof of God's grace and miracles around us.

For example, just look at a gorgeous sunrise with all the magnificent colors. Or the beautiful full moon that shines for miles like a train's light in a tunnel. Or the woman who is diagnosed with life-threatening cancer who returns for a checkup, only to find the tumor is gone. Or the near-miss car accident while driving through the median at 80 mph onto the opposite lane as oncoming traffic is coming toward you, but you call out to Jesus to dodge a head-on collision, and a split-second decision to go back through the median to return to the correct side of the highway occurs without a blowout, rollover, crash or injury of any kind to you, your dog, or anyone else. These are all miracles.

Or how about the fires of Montana in 2018 that burnt 8.8 million acres throughout the summer, and with the state praying, we received three days of snow in the month of September—yes, I said September—which is unheard of and has *never* happened. That, my friend, was a *miracle.*

A miracle is defined in *Webster's New World Dictionary* as "an event or action that appears to contradict known scientific laws and is hence thought to be due to supernatural causes, especially to an act of God."

One more example of miracles around us. I have a friend who had been fighting throat cancer for years and needed to have an eight-hour surgery followed with eight days in the hospital with a tracheotomy and stomach tube until he was stabilized. We called all our praying friends to come together in agreement and prayed with him the night before. We declared and decreed in the mighty name of Jesus that he would walk into the doctor's office the next day and his tumor would be gone. The next day, I received a call and, through the healing power of prayer and God being our great physician and healer, the tumor was gone! Miracles every day and every way!

Every day we wake up and take a breath is a miracle. It doesn't take long looking around us to realize life is a blessing and a gift; that is why it is called the present. We have so many things to be thankful for, and we are blessed.

— ACTION STEPS —

1. Pause for a few minutes and acknowledge when you had faith in a situation that came to pass. Write it down, and give thanks for the faithfulness of our Father in heaven.

2. When have you been in a situation in which you knew that only through God's loving hand could it have had the positive results that it did? Like the

time my friend John had cancer surgery scheduled that miraculously he didn't need as the tumor suddenly was not there anymore. *But God* miracles happen *every day!*

3. Be aware that when you are in a state of fear, there is anxiety, restlessness, distress, inability to sleep, DIS-ease and many more symptoms. When there is faith, there is peace, calmness, and joy. One of my favorite scriptures when I am anxious and fearful is Philippians 4:6–7. This prayer will give you peace beyond understanding every time.

"Be anxious for *nothing,* but in everything with prayer and petition with thanksgiving present your request to God. And the peace of God which surpasses all understanding will guard our hearts and minds in Christ Jesus."

I recommend that, when you find yourself in a stressed, anxious position or experiencing fear, you cleave to a saying, phrase, or scripture that will change your thoughts and calm your mind and heart.

Write down three scriptures as a go-to for renewing your mind.

THE COURAGE TO BE VULNERABLE

WHAT EXACTLY IS being vulnerable?

Vulnerable is defined as "susceptible to physical or emotional attack or harm."

Some of the synonyms are endangered, unsafe, unprotected, exposed, defenseless, and *powerless.* Well, who on earth would want to be vulnerable by these definitions?

In the book *Daring Greatly,* Brené Brown says she defines vulnerability as "uncertainty, risk, and emotional exposure." And when you look at love in regards to this, she states, "It is waking up every day and loving someone who may or may not love us back, whose safety we can't ensure, who may stay in our lives or may leave without a moment's notice, who may be loyal to the day they die or betray us tomorrow—that's vulnerability. Love is uncertain. It's incredibly risky. And loving someone is incredibly risky."

Some people believe being vulnerable is a sign of weakness, when in fact, it is the direct opposite. It takes courage, bravery, valor, boldness, and resolution. I am sure you would agree you would have to stop, ask yourself, and decide if it is really worth it to put yourself out there, to expose yourself, and take the risk.

Without a doubt the answer is yes, yes, and yes!

Why? To set yourself free and to have peace. To live the life you desire. Remember, you have to be vulnerable to experience anything worthwhile or anything worth having.

When we truly trust, believe, and know we were created for greatness, the most important thing to remember is the only opinion that should ever matter to us is that of the one who created us. Let's paint a picture.

You are beautiful and loved unconditionally. The most important person in your life loves you unconditionally through it all, and I mean *all*. The good times, the bad times, the shameful times, the regretful times, the bad choices time, the over-imbibing times, the proud times, the times of no humility, and even the mean or angry times. The list can go on and on, however, we say . . . *But God.*

He knows what we are going to do or say even before we do it or say it. He gives us free will to do what we think may be right, even when we are so wrong in our short-sightedness. Yet, still He loves us and forgives us. He tells us go and sin no more. He knows we will fall again and again. And He is there to pick us up, dust us off, tell us He loves us, that we are the apple of His eye, and that He forgives us and wants us to forgive ourselves so we can live in freedom. We are free to be vulnerable, knowing He will never leave us or forsake us. When you live without a mask, it will set you free.

What an awesome way to live: honestly, in transparency, knowing that we know we are in the process of improving every day, like when we put gold into the fire for processing and it comes out pure and genuine. Or like a tree that is being pruned so the new fruit or branches will blossom and be even more beautiful and fruitful than before.

Another analogy to consider is that iron sharpens iron, which means to make it better, more efficient. In scripture, iron sharpens iron, so a man will sharpen the countenance of his friend.

Trusting during this process is the hardest thing to do because we have to let go of the situation.

Trust is defined by a firm belief in character, strength, or truth of someone who is safe and reliable. Trust is a choice we make every day. It is having a firm belief that the future is bright and that your plan is good and will come to fruition. Psalm 37:4 states, "Delight yourself in the Lord and He will give you the desires of your heart." I have to remind myself and those around me whom I love that while we are in the pruning season or in the fire, this too shall pass and we will come through it better than before with full blossoms and shining more than before.

We are never alone in this process. We have family, friends, community, work relationships, church, and above all of these is our creator, who loves us so unconditionally that He would die for us so we may live and do so in abundance. Jeremiah 29:11 states, "I know the plans I have for you, plans to prosper you and not harm you, plans to give you hope and a future." His plan is perfect and we need to trust Him and know He is faithful in ALL things.

What an amazing picture! We let go of the situation, and we trust that we will get through the process, even though it may hurt or in the fire there will be heat. However, when we get to the other side, there are breakthroughs, purification, healing, strength, and courage to stand in freedom without a mask.

Many experts say there is no testimony without a test. There is no rainbow without the storm or rain. We get to come as we are and rest in the loving arms of our creator. What a comfort in knowing we are protected, loved, and safe. He will be our counselor and give us peace in the process. We are free to be who we are and to be okay with not being okay.

I'm seeing so many people hiding behind masks, literally living in fear of being exposed or judged, and putting on an air that they have got it all together. Reality check . . . there is not a person walking who has not had challenges, crises, health issues, job issues, income issues, families falling apart, abuse issues, or relationships ending. The list is endless. Hopefully that's when we choose to walk in faith, trust, hope, and love, and have mercy and grace for everyone we come into contact with, remembering that we don't know what challenges they are going through at that moment, because until you walk a mile in someone else's shoes there is no room for judgment or comparison. Living with our light on and shining bright for others to see gives them permission to let their light shine. When we "unmask" we can live in the truth and trust God. I love the inspirational message that Marianne Williamson wrote. Everyone needs to see and read it every day:

> "It is our light, not our darkness, that most frightens us. Your playing small does not serve the world. There is nothing enlightened about shrinking so

that others won't feel insecure around you. We ask ourselves, 'Who am I to be brilliant, gorgeous, talented, fabulous?' Actually, who are you not to be? You are a child of God. We are all meant to shine, as children do. We were born to make manifest the glory of God that is within us. It's not just in some of us, it's in everyone and as we let our own light shine, we unconsciously give other people permission to do the same. As we are liberated from our own fear, our presence automatically liberates others."

Therefore, when we are challenged, it is my hope that we would pause. Just pause and look around at the accomplishments we've made and recognize that we aren't where we used to be . . . That we are in forward momentum . . . That it is okay to be transparent and honest with where we've been and where we are headed. God will never lead us where we won't triumph. We must get through the pruning season to have the endless garden of love and light. Look at what pruning does. Some people think pruning is a bad thing, but it is the exact opposite. Pruning is done so there will be more fruit produced from that branch. However, the pruning can be a difficult season due to leaving behind what does not serve you or your future. You must cut off what is dead, or isn't on the same page as you are, or going the same direction. In fact, pruning is defined as "trimming by cutting away dead or overgrown branches or stems, especially to increase fruitfulness and growth"!

What comes to my mind is the scripture Ecclesiastes 3:1–8.

> "For everything there is a season, a time for every purpose under heaven, a time to be born and a time to die; a time to plant and a time to pluck up that which is planted; a time to kill and a time to heal; a time to break down and a time to build up; a time to weep and a time to laugh; a time to mourn and a time to dance; a time to cast away stones and a time to gather stones together; a time to embrace and a time to refrain from embracing; a time to seek and a time to lose; a time to keep and a time to cast away; a time to rend and a time to sew; a time to keep silence and a time to speak; a time to love and a time to hate; a time for war and a time for peace."

What an amazing thing to remember when we are facing something that doesn't feel good. It is just a matter of time before things will change. Nothing stays the same forever. We are either getting better or getting bitter. I encourage you to choose the high road, making constant, never-ending improvement.

We are fully known and loved by our creator. He is faithful to complete His works in us to be all we were created to be. Realize God is not done with you. His plans for you are perfect and good. He promises to provide all the desires of our heart. You may ask, *How do I know that?* Because all our dreams and desires came from Him. Therefore, we should never die with our dreams or music left inside. Being transparent and living in the truth without the mask can be frightening, yet it is also liberating. No more mask! No more faking it till you make it. No more questioning what the story is behind the story. Living in the truth and speaking the truth about your life doesn't make the pain or poor choices you've made go away. Yet there is freedom that comes when you remove the mask. There is no more hiding or living with the facade that everything is perfect. Reality check...nothing is perfect, there is always challenge. In John 16:33 we are told, "I have told you all this so that you may have peace in me. Here on earth you will have many trials and sorrows. But take heart, because I have overcome the world." That is such an encouragement! You no longer have to be captive to the attempt of pretending you have everything together. Like Joyce Meyer states, "Secrets will make us sick and the truth will set us free!" Regardless of whether we hide behind the mask and poor choices of living a lie, the truth always comes out whether we want it to or not. The unbearable shame and pain of living a lie will never set us free. By living unmasked with genuineness, honesty, humbleness, and sincerity, we will be liberated and, therefore, encouraging to others, giving them permission to do the same.

Fear again rears its deceptive head. The battle in our mind kicks into overdrive, and we start believing we won't be forgiven or we are judged. Here's an example and visual for you. Remember in *The Passion of The Christ* by Mel Gibson where the adulteress is on her face groveling at Jesus' feet? All her accusers have circled around her, ready to stone her when Jesus gives them the sign. Much to their surprise, Jesus bends down and writes in the sand while speaking out to the accusers, "If any of you have never sinned, cast the first stone!" When Jesus stands back up, all the accusers have thrown their stones down and left. He then told the adulteress, "They are all gone, you are forgiven, go and sin no more." That example is the most amazing display of the grace of God and unconditional love He has for us. He is our protector and counselor who will put a shield around us at the same time. The realization with the accusers: they who judge not, lest they be judged. Or another favorite truth is, "Let he who lives in a glass house cast the first stone." No one lives in a glass house. No one has not made mistakes, yet we fear and hide behind the mask, hoping no one will notice. The fact is that we *all* are sinners of words, thoughts, and deeds. However, we are forgiven, loved, and accepted unconditionally.

It takes courage to be vulnerable and to walk in truth. This is an amazing way to empower yourself and others to do the same. *Here I am—take me as I am, flawed yet forgiven. I am not where I need to be, and yet grateful I am not where I used to be.* Life is a journey of hills and valleys; we all get to ride the roller coaster, and I would suggest when you're going down that roller coaster of a ride that you throw your hands in the air and enjoy the ride with your hair whipping behind you, knowing that you will be back on top once again. Remember the saying, "Life is either a daring adventure or nothing at all." (Helen Keller) Or how about, "What doesn't kill you makes you stronger." (Friedrich Nietzsche) All fitting in the right situation.

However, I think the best thought for me is, "If God brings us to it, He will bring us through it." He is faithful and is our number one fan. He is so proud of us. He gives us another chance or do-over with freedom of choice. Every door that closes or needs to close is another chance to do things differently. You see, sometimes God's blessings are not in what He gives us but in what He takes away. It's our responsibility to trust Him and to stop trying to pick up what God told us to put down. Do you ever stop and realize that He knows the truth about our future and He's trying to protect us? He knows the beginning from the end. So, when the door closes on a career, a relationship, or a promotion, realize a bigger and better gift and blessing is on the way that He has for you. What looks like rejection is actually God's protection. I encourage you to ask *what* instead of asking *why*. For example, ask God *what* is the lesson He wants you to learn from this. Know that the rejection is not necessarily forever, it could be just for now. But there are red flags that come up and many of us ignore them, thinking it is a fluke. Not true. Call it intuition; I call it the Holy Spirit saying this isn't going to be good. The greatest acknowledgement of a great blessing is when we have peace in mist the of the storm. No anxiety, no stress, no frustration, no anger, no fear. It's God's way of saying, "I've got this, and it is good." Feel the peace, joy, and love of the right and perfect situation. It will expand you instead of contracting you. Trusting in the process, protection, and love of God's plan will bring the best outcome in the long run. Pause, rest, and be still, knowing that all things work out in due time and He has us covered. No more fear! Only love, joy, and peace.

> "My fellow believers, when it seems as though you are facing nothing but difficulties, see it as an invaluable opportunity to experience the greatest joy that you can! For you know that when your faith is tested, it stirs up power within you to endure all things. And then, as your endurance grows even stronger, it will release perfection into every part of your being until there is nothing missing or nothing lacking." (James 1:2–4)

— ACTION STEPS —

1. Define a time when you were vulnerable by being transparent with your feelings or a situation that took courage to step up and speak out. What were the results of this courageous step?

2. When have you ever felt powerless, and what was the situation that surrounded those feelings? Philippians 4:13 states, "I can do all things through Christ who strengthens me." I have used this belief many times as a mantra to say over and over while rocking myself back and forth, like you would a baby in your arms, until peace overcame my mind.

3. Describe one of the most courageous times you experienced in your life. What was happening, and how did you feel when the situation was over?

— — —

Thank you for reading my book. It is an honor and blessing to me. It would mean the world to me if you would write a review from where you purchased it. I hope you will share and recommend my book to your family and friends.

To show my appreciation, I invite you to sign up to receive my free workbook that accompanies my book, UNMASKED. It is my blessing to give this to you.

Please go to www.katy-huff.com/freegift, and I will forward the workbook to your email.

LOVE IS THE WHY

"Love always protects, always trusts, always hopes, always perseveres. Love never fails!" (1 Corinthians 13:7–8)

WE HAVE ALL heard this scripture read at weddings. It is full of what describes the perfect love. Well, I am sure you would agree there's only one perfect and unconditional love. That is, of course, from our God.

"There is no fear in love. But perfect love drives out fear, because fear has to do with punishment. The one who fears is not made perfect in love." (1 John 4:18)

What we need to realize is faith and fear cannot co-exist. When we live in fear, we are always thinking about an unpleasant or frightening event, or have a scarcity mentality, which causes fear to rear its ugly head. We have to take our thoughts captive and take control of where our mind is going. When we pause to reflect and stop hiding behind the mask, we then will have the best chance of setting ourselves free and breaking the chains of that bondage. Webster's definition of bondage is "the state of being a slave, being physically restrained, as by being tied up, chained or in handcuffs." When you take the mask off, you will set yourself free.

The truth will set us free: free to take the mask off, and free to live a life of love. Free to be, do, and have all that we ever wanted without anything or anyone holding us back. When we come to realize that love is the answer, there is no need to hide behind the mask.

Remember in the earlier chapter where we discussed unconditional love? That is what we have when we realize who we are . . . a child of God, and whose we are . . . the child of a God who has taken away and forgiven us for all our mistakes, failures, short-comings. He loves us so much that there is nothing we can ever do that He hasn't already forgiven us for. His love for us is so overwhelming. He has said, "I have loved you with an everlasting love." Joyce Meyers repeatedly states, "He will never love us more than He does right now." It's the most ever, it's unconditional, it is without boundaries, and it is not based on what you have or have not done! That is, by the way, *unconditional love*. It is given freely to us; 1 John 3:1 states, "See what great love the Father has lavished on us, that we should be called children of God!" That is exactly what we are! Children of God. What parent would not take a bullet or step in front of a moving car to save their child? Well, that's what He has done for us. He has died for us so that we could live free with grace and forgiven without guilt, shame, or condemnation. So, doesn't it make sense for us to forgive ourselves so we can live free without fear, shame, guilt, and condemnation? The love He gives us is not based on what we have done or what we haven't done. It is freely given to us. When we consciously chose to live in faith with unconditional love, it will set us free and that, my friends, is beyond all comprehension. All He asks is for us to love Him with all our heart, our soul, and all our mind, putting Him first above everything else. Seek Him first, His kingdom and righteousness, and all things will be granted unto us. (Mathew 6:33) Simple things to adopt and live by: reach for Him in good times, bad times, all times.

First, He's our biggest fan, greatest supporter, and number one cheerleader who wants only the best for us. He comforts us, protects us, counsels us, and provides for us. Ephesians 3:20 says, "Now to see Him who is able to do immeasurably more than all we ask or imagine, according to His power that is at work within us." Wow! Can you just imagine that He can and will do above and beyond all that we ask? Let that settle deep inside you. Do you have your number one supporter saying to you: "I know your dreams and desires because I placed them inside you. Yet, I am going to do even more than you asked for or it will be more than you can ever imagine!" A very simplistic example of this is asking for one thousand dollars, and He gives you a billion dollars instead. Immeasurably more than all we could ever ask or imagine. Such unconditional love, provision, and victory in our lives. When you ask for something and it doesn't come through, it can be that it is out of His will for the plan, or His plan is exceedingly bigger.

Secondly, He asks us to love our neighbors like ourselves and to love each other as He has loved us. John 15:30 states, "There is no greater love than this: to lay down one's life for one's friends." A friend loves at all times. It's truly very simple. Number one, love God. Number two, love each other!

Love is the answer. Live in the light, and show up without a mask. Be secure in who you are and let your light shine. Know that you are loved unconditionally. He knows your flaws, He created you. He has forgiven you, and He wants you to live free. Live knowing it is well with your soul, and you are loved. Love is the why, it truly is the answer.

What does it look like to live with your arms wide open without a mask? It can look so many different ways. For some, it can feel very scary or risky to be vulnerable. There can be a lot of fear in exposing the true inner being that we are with all our fears, showing our faults, facades, mistakes, bad decisions, hurts, pain, and betrayals, and feeling judged or condemned for them. Because of those emotions that popped up in their heads in the middle of the journey toward living a life with arms wide open and without any more masks, many may feel intimidated by the fear of judgment and so many other negative connotations.

But what if you could look at it differently? What if we decided to change that channel in our heads to hear it differently and look, feel, see, smell, and touch our hearts in such a glorious, freeing position that we were unstoppable? What if we could remove the piano from our backs with all the baggage that we have been carrying for days, weeks, or even years? It would be so freeing that it could feel like you have lost one hundred pounds. Consider this statement by Cesare Pavese: "If you wish to travel far and fast, travel light."

Let go of the past and the baggage. It is gone forever and there is no-thing that we can do or say to make it be different. We tend to beat ourselves up for things that will never change. However, we can do things differently in the future. "Take off all the envies, jealousies, comparisons, unforgiveness, shame, and selfishness." (Cesare Pavese)

I want to encourage you to take off the burdens you were never intended to bear.

You know that you know:

- **You were created in the image of the only perfect person ever.**

  "So God created man in His own image; in the image of God He created him." (Genesis 1:27)

- **You are a child of God.**

  "The Father has loved us so much that we are called children of God. And we really are His children." (1 John 3:1)

  "I will be a Father to you, and you will be my sons and daughters, says the Lord Almighty." (2 Corinthians 6:18)

- **You were created to have a life of abundance.**

  "I have come so that they may have life and they may have it more abundantly." (John 10:10)

- **You are loved unconditionally.**

  "We know how much God loves us, and we have put our trust in His love. God is love, and all who live in love live in God, and God lives in them." (1 John 4:16)

- **You are protected and will always be provided for.**

"And my God will meet all your needs according to the riches of His glory in Christ Jesus." (Philippians 4:19)

"The Lord is my shepherd; I shall not want." (Psalm 23:1)

"When we have faith, it is an assurance of things hoped for and evidence of things not seen." (Hebrews 11:1)

- **His plans for us are good.**

"For I know the plans I have for you, plans for peace and well-being, not to harm but to give you hope and a future." (Jeremiah 29:11)

- **We can be strong and courageous.**

"Since we have such hope and confident expectation, we speak with great courage." (2 Corinthians 3:12)

- **There is no fear in walking in the truth of who we are.**

"Then you will know the truth and the truth will set you free." (John 8:32)

- **We can walk with arms wide open without a mask being true to who we are.**

"For God did not give us a spirit of timidity or fear or cowardice but of power and of love and of sound judgment and personal judgment." (2 Timothy 1:7)

- No more anxiety to be the real you.

  "Do not be anxious for anything but in everything by prayer and petition with thanksgiving present your requests to God. And the peace of God which transcends all understanding will guard your heart and mind." (Philippians 4:6)

We have nothing—or *no-thing*—to worry about because the peace will guard our hearts and minds.

You have to have some elements of courage and peace knowing we have a guard around us, protecting us, and providing for us. That's so powerful to imagine there is a man, our Father, who loves us unconditionally, with all our faults, who has forgiven and, better yet, forgotten all our mistakes. He loves us so much that He died for us to give us grace and mercy every day of our lives. Picture that, if you can. The beautiful love that is only experienced from our Father in heaven.

He sees us as priceless! We are *worthy!*

So, when you know this, not just in your head but also in your heart, you have no reason to fear the truth of who you are and whose you are. He puts the shield of protection around you every day, every minute, and every second of your life. You are safe in the arms of Jesus. No one can touch you. You are safe, loved, and adored.

So, I'd like to ask you to humor me for a minute. Just imagine that you have one child. You absolutely love this child with your whole being unconditionally. However, you know you have to give them up to save the world. You know how their life will be, how they will be treated, and how they will lose their life. There will be verbal attacks, physical attacks, and slander. They will be disparaged, accused of things that make them a criminal in society, and finally, executed based on rumors, lies, and allegations. Their death will not be easy. They are going to be spit on, hit in the face, tortured, and whipped with hooks that would tear their hide and rip their muscles out of their back. They will wear a crown of thorns that will be pressed into their skull, causing them to have excruciating pain and bleeding. They will carry a huge cross without help until they cannot carry on. Only then will someone assist them, and at the end, they will be stripped of their clothing, then nails will be pounded through their hands and their feet to a cross, and then they will be scoffed at, spit on, stabbed inside of their ribs and tortured—all because this plan for their life is to set the rest of the world free from our mistakes, our sins, our faults, our shame, and our condemnation. Your child would go through hell and die to save the rest of the world. They would die so that we could live. Can you or would you be able to stand back, knowing what's to come for your child because of the most beautiful unconditional love that will be given to the world? Could you do it? Could you sacrifice your one and only child for the call on their life to set us all free? When I think of this, I am so overwhelmed. It affects me at the heart level like nothing else. There is no other man that will ever love us more. That type of unconditional love is so foreign to most of us. To love the world so much that you give up your one and only child you have. Wow! I am not sure how anyone could stand by watching this unfold and not want to scream, *STOP! Stop all of this!* To step in and save your one and only child is what most parents would do.

Talk about unconditional love that is amazing, awesome, and selfless. The ultimate gift to the world. That your child would die to set everyone else free is the ultimate, unconditional, unfathomable love. So beautiful, so powerful that His call on His life was to set us all free.

At times, it makes me feel unworthy that someone would die so I would be set free to live without a mask, forgiven, given grace, and loved. That no mistake is too big or bad to be forgiven and, more importantly, forgotten. So, doesn't it make sense for us to forget and forgive ourselves so we can live with our arms wide open? We have been forgiven and are loved. Therefore, we should also extend the same love, forgiveness, and grace to others. We have had the *best* example of forgiveness, tolerance, acceptance, and pure love. This has been the most awesome opportunity to live with our arms wide open, just as the example that was shown to us. Therefore, we are *free!*

FREE to be all that we have been created to be.

FREE to be true to who we are.

FREE to live without guilt.

FREE to live without shame or condemnation.

FREE to be authentic and live with integrity.

FREE to live fearlessly and with courage.

FREE to love unconditionally and to have unconditional love.

FREE to be vulnerable, knowing we are loved, forgiven, and accepted, and therefore, to live in peace.

FREE to live without a mask!

It is my prayer and wish that as you take off your mask and have the courage to do so, that you will feel free, empowered, and at peace . . . That you will feel confident and secure to live with your arms wide open with peace, love, and faith in who you are designed to be . . . That you have faith in the fact that you are a precious child of God and you were born in the image of an almighty king, a great counselor, the good shepherd, the Prince of Peace.

If only we had an ironclad belief and knowing that we each have a perfect plan designed for each of us, then the worry and fear would no longer exist. If we knew without a shadow of a doubt that the divine plan is for success, then we would trust everything that happens. How many times have you had a conversation with someone and you discussed that everything happens for a reason? I know for myself there are times it can be daily, especially when we are living in one lane and then suddenly everything changes. For instance, you lose a job, a family member dies, your relationship ends with the love of your life, you lose your home, you are diagnosed with a serious illness, or many, many other examples could be used here. Everything changes. We ask the question, "Why me?" instead of thinking we are being protected from something that would be detrimental. The perfect plan didn't include that road. The road to the right or left has a better outcome that is safer and healthier that would get you closer to becoming the best you and having what is best for you. When you come to a place that when you are fighting or forcing something to happen, it rarely ever works out for the best. If there isn't peace in the efforts, then maybe it is a sign to let go, to release it and trust that what is meant to be will be.

I remember being given advice about a situation I had with a relationship that went bad. The advice given to me that was this:

> "Do not follow through with what is on your heart. And if you do, it will be like a kite crashing into the ground into a million little pieces."

Well, sure enough, I did just that: I chose to follow through with what was on my heart and showed up at the wrong time and at the wrong place. It was not good. The lessons we learn can be easy and gentle or hard like a hit with a brick. Some of us, myself included, take many hits before the lesson is learned. I'm happy to say I am done with that particular lesson, and I've got the scars to show from it. Now when things don't go like I think they should, I pause, reflect, and believe there's something better. It is in the waiting that we get clarity, peace, and answers. It is God's way of protecting me.

> "Trust in the Lord with all your heart and lean not on your own understanding, in all ways acknowledge Him and He will make your path straight." (Proverbs 3:5–6)

It's not the right time, right place, right person, right position—and it's okay! There is something or someone better, safer, more supportive for me. Just like that analogy of the square peg forced into the round hole not working very well. In fact, it doesn't work at all. I say all that to point out we all are in our own process and journey. But we all are dealing with some issues that can cause us to rise or fall. Choose rising. Choose love, light, and life. Say no to the slow bleed. For instance, I had a friend say to me that when we continue to pick at the scab (i.e., the situation), it continues to bleed. Let it heal, and let it go.

We will all have trials and tribulations; what we do with them will either bring life or death. Chose life. Do we surrender with the white flag waving or do we say that this too shall pass?

Chose peace in the mists of a storm.

> Deuteronomy 30:19 states, "I call heaven and earth to witness against you today, that I have set before you life and death, blessing and curse. Therefore, choose life, that you and your offspring may live."

The example of looking for love in all the wrong places is similar to cake. I bet you are questioning what cake has to do with anything.

Well, there is frosting and then the cake. For those who are wanting an immediate result, they go for the frosting. Get your sugar rush, creating an absolute fill of excitement with the high sugar levels in your blood. That is giving you a steep peak of energy and an amazing high. Euphoria! Only when the sugar is absorbed, you then have the crash to a very low sugar level. Now you're feeling sick, tired, lethargic, depressed, or down. Or better yet, you get to see it, and look in the mirror seeing the results of the sugar that we carry on our bodies as a reminder of that euphoric, short-lived time. Alternatively, you can wait for the cake to bake, the foundation, and have some of the frosting with the cake. Now you can "have your cake and eat it too" with sugar levels being balanced versus the peak and trough—you can have the complete piece of cake. The rewarding long-lasting sugar level, or in this case, the meaningful, unconditional loving, committed relationship, will last a lot longer than the sugar rush. So, the conscious choice we need to make is the sugar rush, immediate gratification or the long-standing, long-lasting relationship with a genuine, meaningful, unconditionally loving relationship. Choosing quality, long-lasting, fulfilling, respectful, loving relationships will last forever.

Obviously, the choice is ours; God gives us free choice. A dear sweet friend asked what's wrong with having the rush, living in the moment with the "sins of the flesh," and repenting at the end of her life, asking God to forgive her, would she not be forgiven? The answer is yes! Absolutely, she would of course be forgiven. Yet, how empty and short-lived the frosting is, the shame and feeling broken versus having a deep, intimate, long-lasting, quality, unconditional loving, respectful, honoring, cherishing, priceless relationship. Do you want quality or quantity? These choices we get to make on a daily basis. Will there be challenges? Of course. However, when you build a relationship or a house on sand, it will crash, but one built on rocks, the one and only rock, will weather the storms. That rock is the God way, not my way. What people don't remember is when we bottom out from the sugar rush, we then get flooded with the terrible feeling of being unloved, unworthy, ashamed, lonely, and at times, even dirty. We need to take a pause and remember again we are a child of a king. That His plan for us is so good. That it's an Ephesian 3:20 moment:

> "Now to Him who is able to do super abundantly more than all that we dare, ask or think, infinitely beyond our greatest prayers, hopes or dreams, according to His power that is at work within us, to him be the glory in the church and in Christ Jesus throughout all generations forever and ever AMEN!"

Therefore, why settle for being a pawn when you were created as a queen or king for greatness? Every one of us was created for the greatness within us, and we are royalty, so why would we settle for less? I want to encourage you to treat yourself as a daughter of a king, royalty, and treat your body as a temple. Know that when you take the shortcut or reach for the rush, it can be like a kite crashing to the ground, broken in a million pieces. There is no long-term satisfaction, no peace or feeling contented, respected, adored, or even loved in the shortcuts or with the sugar rush. You deserve to be cherished, honored, loved, and respected. Remember, you matter and you deserve to be valued.

— ACTION STEPS —

1. How would you describe what love is? When have you experienced or received it? What were your feelings at that time in receiving love?

2. 1 Corinthians 13:1–7 defines what love is; write it out and review it every day.

3. How we live our lives every day in love is the why. We reap what we sow; therefore, we should treat others like we would want to be treated. That's the Golden Rule! When was there a time that you reached out to someone in love? What did it look like? What feelings did you experience after you showed someone love or were present to support them?

NO MISTAKES HERE

You don't make mistakes.

Our Father in heaven knew us when we were in the womb. "Indeed, the very hairs on your head are all numbered. Don't be afraid; you are worth more." (Luke 12:7) He knows every hair on our heads, and He promised His plan for us is perfect. In fact, from the moment we were created, He had our future already mapped out.

We were told that there would be trials and tribulations; however, according to Hebrews 13:6, "The Lord is my helper, I will not fear. What can man do to me?" He overcame the world, and this challenge or roadblock that we may be experiencing will also pass. Every day, all day, we need to be in conversations with God, praying without ceasing because the power of prayer is real. Pray that we are able to hear His voice and to have our spirit to lead us in everything. Trust that He knows our plans and future, and *it is good!*

Still being the loving, patient Father that He is, He gives us *free will* and free choice to do what we feel and want at any moment. He is a gentleman and would never force our hand. In fact, He is jealous for our love. This is the greatest gift He could have given us and also the greatest pain we would receive. Sometimes we want instant gratification, better known as living in the flesh, and think *if it feels good . . . do it!* Then we will end up with the loneliness, guilt, shame, and feeling unworthy, all for the excitement of the moment, only to have to look in the mirror and ask ourselves, *What have I done?* Believing that our plan would be better than the ultimate gift or plan that our Father had for us is so shortsighted on our part. How could we not love and respect ourselves enough to believe what our Father and our protector would want is *best* for us in that moment? To honor and respect ourselves is to wait for the man that will adore, cherish, respect, and honor us. Once again, we find ourselves broken, hurt, suffering, and struggling due to our possible impatience, selfishness, greed, pride, or other feelings that lead us astray.

Our feelings and emotions are like the weather; give it fifteen minutes and it will change. Living life according to our emotions is a train wreck waiting to happen, leading us on the notorious rollercoaster ride or the adrenaline rush that comes to a crashing end. We then look in the mirror and see the scars from the backlash of jumping in front of God's perfect plan for our lives and see remorse, shame, and questioning. When there isn't peace, that is our sign to stop the madness before it ever starts . . . so, *here's your sign!* Anxiety, stress, DIS-ease (which leads to sickness), shame, and no peace. Shame is defined as a "painful feeling of humiliation or distress caused by the consciousness of wrong or foolish behavior." This is what happens when we settle and make a choice to live in the moment for immediate gratification only to walk away with the residual effects of bad choices.

By the way, God knows we are going to make those decisions even before we carry them out. He gives us free will and knows us intimately. However, when we settle, we give up part of who we are and what we were called to be, do, and have in His eyes. Yet His plans for us are good. Plans to prosper us and not harm us. Plans for hope and a future. (Jeremiah 29:11) He guards us and protects us. He forgives us and will set us free.

Give thanks to God for all He does, for providing us with peace in all things. When we give our past, present, and future to Him through our prayers and conversations with Him and ask Him to take them away, then we are clean and forgiven. Our hearts and minds are washed clean, set free. That, my friend, is when you take a timeout and listen to your spirit and soul, better known as your holy spirit or your intuition. It is there for a reason—to be the little voice of reason and a positive support to lead you.

I want you to know without a shadow of doubt that the past is the past. It is gone and there is absolutely nothing we can do about it. As you see, no-thing can be done. When we focus on the past, it only keeps those emotions stirred up. Stirring a pot of goo only thickens it, which means those shameful, anxious, hurtful, sad, negative feelings rear their ugly heads and do not serve you.

> "Be anxious for nothing but through prayers and petitions, with thanksgiving, present your request to God. And the peace of God which transcends all understanding will guard your hearts and minds." (Philippians 4:6–7)

> "Trust in the Lord with all your heart and lean not on your own understanding. In all ways, acknowledge Him and He shall direct thy path." (Proverbs 3:5–6)

Reading and repeating these scriptures will inevitably bring peace to your heart and mind and, therefore, set you free. We can only live in the present; as the experts say, it is a gift. Make decisions today based on the plan for us being perfect. Always make decisions based on long-term happiness and not only in the moment.

Due to these verses, we must believe that the plan for us is the very best plan that we could ever dream or imagine so we could be all that we want, do all that we want, or have all that we want. It is at a time like this that we would reflect and ask for our spirit to lead us. His timing is not our timing. So,

When we hear "It's wrong," we say NO.

When we hear "Release," we let GO.

When we hear "Walk away," then we leave.

If He says "Be still," then we will wait.

If He says "Trust," then we will obey.

Pray that He will teach us how to follow in His ways. For He is the truth, the way, and the life, so therefore proclaim, *"I am done chasing feelings."* Make a conscious choice to have your spirit lead you instead of the emotions of the moment. Feelings will lead you down a rabbit hole you won't want to be in.

Trusting and believing in His perfect plan is critical to your peace and freedom. Free to live *on purpose with passion* for being the best you that you were created to be. We must learn to trust God, especially when we don't see Him. By doing so, we can live at a level ten in our gifts.

What I have found is there are no mistakes. Everything does happen for a reason, and the lessons are every day. There will be tests in this life, and they happen to create a testimony. The bottom line is our mess will become our message. Therefore, our messes and tests are going to be such an encouragement for others to see and believe that with God all things are possible. That He is our protector and provider even when we choose our free will.

We become the person we need to be through the tests and messes that sculpt us into the person we were created to be, so that others will come to know they are not alone. With each experience, we can survive and, in many situations, thrive, giving us all reassurance. I want to encourage you to aspire to live a life with your arms wide open in support of others. The fear of surrendering can sometimes look like the largest mountain one will ever climb in their life. Yet it all starts with one step at a time, one day at a time. With constant and never-ending progress, we will arrive on the top of the mountain. Looking over the valley and the beautiful scenery from that summit will take our breath away. The awe-inspiring, breathtaking, miraculous vision from the top will be more than we can ever imagine. As the saying goes, *I can only imagine . . .*

What a celebration it will be to know that we have arrived, that we, too, can overcome any trials that come our way. What I continually hear is, *Peace, be still and know I am God*. It is so much easier to surrender all, with hope and faith, than to fight the battle especially when we choose to do it alone. We think we are alone due to the choices we have made through free will, when we should instead be trusting, believing, and knowing without a shadow of a doubt that we are never alone and that we can, at any time, step into our greatness and live a life of peace and truth of who we are. We can choose to live with courage and to be vulnerable, which gives us power to be *unmasked and free!*

We are His reflection; He has created us in His image. He doesn't make mistakes, and He surely didn't start with you. Even though we may fall or falter, I know and hope you come to know that we are not far from where we were called to be. We must trust that His plan for us is unique and perfect for us, which is all that we desire. I will not pretend that I know better than He does. After all, He loves me unconditionally.

We look to others to feel approval, and we long for validation by how many people are following us on social media or how many likes we get. However, who we are came from God. My identity is that I am a child of God. The truth will ultimately set me, and you, free. What others say about me does not define me. Therefore, I won't waste another day believing words that God didn't say.

There is a scripture that states, "And even the very hairs of your head are all numbered. So don't be afraid." (Matthew 10:30–31) He chooses us every day, every minute, and every second of our lives, waiting for us to surrender and be *free.*

See, the *overwhelming, never-ending, reckless love of God* is there always and forever unconditionally. He gives us free will to make the decisions we feel are right, but He will chase us down, and never leave us or forsake us. He accepts us even with our flaws. We couldn't earn His love, and at times we don't even deserve it, yet His overwhelming, never-ending, reckless love is always there, *always!* He is waiting with His arms wide open for us to return to Him. He loves us so much that there is not a mountain He wouldn't climb. He would walk through fire for us, and there is no lie He won't tear down coming after us. His love is never-ending, unconditional, and beyond our wildest imaginations. Can you feel it?

"Can you Feel It?" by Angela Pinkston

There are melodies of eternity

Woven into the fabric of time

Age old harmonies creation has seen

From the first dawning of light

Do you hear it?

Sounds of beauty Divine

Can you feel it?

In the story of your life

There are hidden dreams kept in realms unseen

Eager for the moment they're found

Keys of destiny cut for royalty

Who will journey past all doubt

Do you hear it?

Sounds of beauty Divine

Can you feel it?

In the story of your life

Do you hear it?

Voice of wonders Divine

Can you feel it?

Awakening your life

We were meant for greatness

Kept for such a time as this

Made from love, made to fly

Born to change the course of life

Do you her it?

Sounds of beauty divine

Can you feel it?

This paragraph I said before and bears repeating as a reminder of the perfect plan and encouragement for us: "Setback is a setup for a comeback. If God showed you all that He has planned for you, it would boggle your mind. If you could see the doors He's going to open, the opportunities that will cross your path, and the people who will show up, you'd be so amazed, excited and passionate, it would be so easy to set your mind for victory. That is what faith is all about. You've got to believe it before you see it. God's favor is surrounding you like a shield. Every setback is a set up for a comeback! Every bad break, every disappointment and every person who does you wrong is part of the plan to get you to where you are supposed to be." (Anonymous)

"So don't lose your bold, courageous faith for you are destined for a great reward." (Hebrews 10:35)

"My fellow believers, when it seems as though you are facing nothing but difficulties, see it as an invaluable opportunity to experience the greatest joy that you can! For you know that when your faith is tested it stirs up power within you to endure all things. And then as your endurance grows even stronger it will release perfection into every part of your being until there is nothing missing or nothing lacking." (James 1:2–4)

TIMING IS EVERYTHING!

I AM A POSTER child for His perfect timing.

> "If it seems slow, do not despair, for these things will surely come to pass. Just be patient! They will not be overdue a single day!" (Habakkuk 2:3)

So true! I was raised in a community that placed huge value on perseverance, tenacity, and don't-stop-believing, take-the-bull-by-the-horns attitudes. Much like a dog on a bone, pushing through versus resting and trusting. It is a daily walk to trust that we don't have to take the bull by the horns. When we surrender all to the one who has created us for greatness and loves us beyond our wildest dreams, there is so much freedom and peace in knowing, in trusting that at the right time when you are ready for that next relationship or that next promotion in your career, or the next chapter of your life, it will surely come to pass. It is amazing when you surrender and trust God's plan and timing for your life, miracles happen. Let me give you a personal example.

I was praying and waiting for my desires to come to fruition with the man that I felt I was meant to be with. I prayed for him to become a Christian and for our relationship to be restored. I labored, prayed, pursued, fasted, and enlisted others to come along side me for this man, lamenting and pushing things for two years. As I said earlier, God gives us free will, yet we have to trust that sometimes we are being protected from a terrible mistake. So that is where we must rest and wait patiently. When you least expect it, the plan comes through divinely and suddenly in a mic-drop moment. Let me explain.

I had a friend that was a counselor and pastor. He was there to counsel me through my heartbreak. While this was happening to me, his dead-end marriage eroded. We became best friends and did everything together. We would attend sporting events, go snowshoeing, watch movies, and go to concerts, church, restaurants . . . we did basically everything together, but always as friends. I would introduce him as my BFF, Best Friend Forever. Then all of a sudden, right after I told a friend I wasn't interested or looking for a relationship, she warns me and says, "Well, brace yourself because that is usually when it will show up." Within two weeks when my friendship had shifted apart, I had a clear message come to me that said "Let no man separate what I have put together." Oh my gosh . . . *really!* I had been praying for an Ephesians 3:20 man to come into my life.

> Ephesians 3:20 states, "Now to Him who is able to carry out His purpose and do superabundantly more than all we dare to ask or think, infinitely beyond our greatest prayers, hopes or dreams, according to His power that is at work within us, to Him be the glory in the church and in Christ Jesus throughout all generations forever and ever. AMEN!"

Here stood the man who had been my best friend for two years, who God had put in my path, is everything I could have ever dreamed for and beyond. I mean everything! Timing is everything! Two years ago, I wouldn't have even seen who this amazing man was, due to where I was in my own life experience. I wasn't ready for all that He had for me. This amazing friend, who is everything I could have ever asked for, is beyond all my hopes and dreams.

I tell you this because sometimes we think we know better than the perfect plan and calling on our life. However, when we trust in all things to work out for our highest good, in the perfect timing at the perfect place as long as we wait in good courage, He will strengthen our heart. Psalm 20:4 says, "May He grant your hearts desires and make all your plans succeed!"

Trust is defined as "firm belief in the reliability, truth, ability, or strength of someone or something." So timing is crucial. Don't be impatient. Keep traveling steadily along, and in due time you will be honored with every blessing, desire, wish, and plan that has been put inside you so you can live out your calling and purpose that you deserve and desire. Isaiah 60:22 states, "When the right time comes, I will make this happen quickly. I am the Lord!" Grateful for the promises we have and blessed to be an example of His timing and answers to prayer. Just trust in His timing and plans for your life.

If you are pushing something and feel resistance, anxiety, or frustration in a relationship, career, or anything, you may want to stop. Focus on what you're feeling. If there is peace, you are on the right path; if not, the timing may not be right. Wait patiently, trusting that, if not this, then something or someone better is part of His plan. As Dave Meyers says, "Cast your cares and rest in Him, and at the right time it will surely come to pass."

HOW TO REMOVE THE MASK
and LIVE FREE

I**T IS MY HOPE** that by now you are realizing that you no longer have to hide behind a mask.

No more:

- settling
- shame
- self-betrayal
- feeling unworthy
- hiding

There are five steps you are going to want to implement so you will live in confidence knowing that you are blessed, loved, accepted, worthy, and priceless.

STEP 1

Know that you are royalty in the eyes of God, that His plan for you is perfect, that you are the apple of His eye.

Proclaim out loud and create index cards with these truths for you to read every day!

I AM . . .

A daughter of the King. (Galatians 3:26)

Altogether beautiful and fair, there is NO flaw in me. (Song of Songs 4:7)

Steadfast in the love of God. (Romans 8:31–38)

Redeemed. (Ephesians 1:7)

Loved. (Isaiah 43:3)

Beautiful. (Psalm 139:13–16)

Free. (John 8:36)

Strong and courageous. (Joshua 1:9)

Transformed. (Romans 12:2)

Favored. (Proverbs 22:11)

Joyful. (John 15:11)

Victorious. (Philippians 4:13)

At peace. (John 14:27)

STEP 2

Consider starting a journal to document your journey to living free and stepping into the future with a new vision of who you are and whose you are. Write out a plan of what your vision is for your next chapter of living unmasked and celebrating your transformation.

STEP 3

Reach out to two or three people that you trust and have your best interest at heart who could become support persons and cheerleaders for your new chapter of living free. Set an expectation with them to encourage you in this journey.

STEP 4

Consider burning all the feelings you have harbored that caused you to wear a mask in the first place. What that means is to take a piece of paper and write on it the negative thoughts or accusations you have had spoken to you, fears, limiting beliefs like, "I can't . . . I am not . . ." and burn the paper so you never will have to see or believe that this is truth. Then, repeat step one again filling yourself with truth and love.

STEP 5

Finally, use the P.U.S.H. process when you are stuck. That is to *Pray Until Something Happens.*

CONCLUSION

I WANT TO say how grateful that I am that you have taken the time to read this book. I hope that it will bless you beyond your wildest dreams and for many years of living unmasked and free. It is my prayer that you will choose to not "fake it till you make it" but to "faith it till you make it" and be set free. Therefore, you will move from broken to blessed by living in hope and faith with courage to be vulnerable and live with freedom, peace, and love. You will live with your arms wide open. Trust and believe that you have a calling on your life that is perfect for you, with all the ups and downs, the good times and bad, and know you are loved unconditionally through the total journey we are on, which is called life.

My hope is now that you have read this book, you have a better understanding of knowing. John 16:33 states that "In this world you will have troubles. But take courage, I have overcome the world." You are never alone; He will never leave you or forsake you, therefore, you can have peace in the storms of your life.

Your next step is to step up and out boldly. Stand with the courage to be vulnerable, living in the truth of who you are and whose you are. Know deep within your head, heart, and total being that you are free to be and there is *no* reason to live behind a mask. You will know you are free when the fruits of the spirit—love, joy, peace, patience, kindness, goodness, faithfulness, gentleness, and self-control—are apparent in your life. (Galatians 5:22–23)

I hope that you will take a moment to rate this book, tweet, and share about it on Facebook in hopes that it will help others who need to learn how to live **UNMASKED** and **FREE,** knowing they are loved unconditionally.

God bless you and keep you.
Living life with my arms wide open,
Loving God and Loving people.

HUGS,
Katy Huff

To contact Katy, reach her at:
Katyhuffrn@gmail.com
Katyhuffrn on Instagram
katy-huff.com

Thank you for reading my book. It is an honor and blessing to me. It would mean the world to me if you would write a review from where you purchased it. I hope you will share and recommend my book to your family and friends.

To show my appreciation, I invite you to sign up to receive my free workbook that accompanies my book, *UNMASKED*. It is my blessing to give this to you.

Please go to
www.katy-huff.com/freegift
and I will forward the workbook to your email.

ABOUT THE AUTHOR

Katy Huff BSN, RN, is a daughter, wife, sister, aunt, friend, and small-town girl who has traveled internationally with many ministries and is a sought-after speaker and corporate trainer. Katy has hosted women's retreats for over 10 years, speaking truth into and encouraging women to step into their greatness of who they are and to live an intentional, divinely orchestrated life. Her transparency and passion empower others to be, do and have all that they were created to be. Katy has participated in prophetic training at Christian International in Santa Rosa. Katy is married to David and they live on a lake in Montana, where they enjoy outdoor activities and are very involved in their church and healing ministry.

Made in the USA
Middletown, DE
29 October 2021